20

Smoking Food

Acknowledgments

There are many people who can cook but few are great chefs! I like to be the cook, to always be learning and open to new ideas and techniques, but I would not be able to feed my passion for cooking without the close support of my wife Tina and my family, Kacey and Holly. Tina, this book is about all the times I have set off the smoke alarms; and Kacey and Holly, my culinary assistants at the grand ages of seven and three, I look forward to the future when you will be the king and queen of the grill. Thanks also to Nancy and Lou McNabb, always in good faith; and to June Fortune and the late Jack Fortune, my thoughts are always with you. To my brother Gavin Fortune and father Ken Fortune who keeps the barbecue fires burning, and always in memory of my twin brother Jeremy Fortune who passed away in May 2007 — "and nothing else matters."

Most of all, support your regional food producers, buy locally made and taste the real New Zealand.

Text © Chris Fortune, 2010
Typographical design © David Bateman Ltd, 2010

Published in the United States by
STACKPOLE BOOKS
5067 Ritter Road
Mechanicsberg, PA 17055
www.stackpolebooks.com

ISBN 978-0-8117-1442-6

First published in 2010 by David Bateman Ltd,
30 Tarndale Grove, Albany, Auckland, New Zealand
www.batemanpublishing.co.nz

Book design: Alice Bell
Photographs: all photographs by Jock "the camera" and Chris Fortune, except
    pp 15, 19, 27, 31 (all), 33 (all), 36, 39, 47 48, 51, 55, 59, 60, 61, 63, 64, 71 & 89
    (Dreamstime Photo Library); pp 5, 6, 11, 24, 28, 34, 40, 55 (all), 59 (all) & 84
    (iStock)
Illustrations: pp 44–45, Nicki Lowe, Vanilla Fish Design
Printed in China through Colorcraft Ltd, Hong Kong

Smoking Food

A GUIDE TO SMOKING MEAT, FISH & SEAFOOD, VEGETABLES, CHEESE, NUTS AND OTHER TREATS

CHRIS FORTUNE

STACKPOLE
BOOKS

Contents

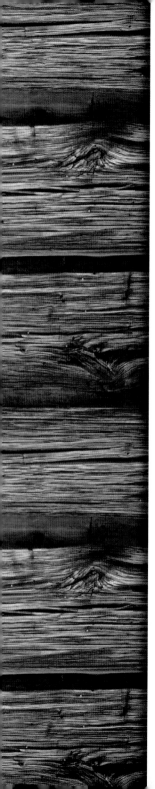

RECIPES:
BASIC & ADVENTUROUS

GETTING STARTED

Introduction

Are you a "taster"? Do you experiment with cooking techniques, food products and the way you gather ingredients for the dinner table? Are you willing to step outside the ordinary and taste, test then tempt others to try something new? Is a culinary challenge of the smoky kind one you'd accept? If you answered yes to even one of these questions then you're reading the right book.

Our food tastes are very much determined by our anatomy, who we are, our culture and by how hungry we are for the next dinner! You may be satisfied by simple, everyday tastes or by more complex flavors that you've developed in your own cooking over time. This book will help you create more of both of those types of tastes — it offers basic information about smoking and smoked products and presents a suite of delicious, more complex recipes that can be followed word for word or, for the more adventurous cook, modified to especially treat your palate.

Times have changed. The way we cook has changed and the way we prepare and process our foods also has — more so over the last 50 years than the last 2000. The invention of refrigeration allows every household to stock great quantities of perishable items at a constant temperature until they are needed. Think about what we would do if we had no chillers or freezers. What did your great-grandparents do and does that resemble the way we forage, gather and hunt for our weekly shop today? Well it might for some of us. Even if "foraging" and "hunting" are not part of your vocabulary, those actions are, still, part of your weekly shopping trip when you enter the aisles at the supermarket, lined full-length with –6°F freezers and 25°F chiller units.

These stark containers illuminate vacuum-packed chicken and beef products, accentuate the uniformness of boneless and nameless pork and lamb cuts, and hide the fact that not so long ago we enjoyed a more intimate relationship with what we ate.

To smoke food, either to flavor or to preserve it, is to go back to the basics — to a time when food was stored for future days of the week or different seasons of the year. Products such as bacon, smoked hams and salamis are now mainstream and the reason they were smoked is mostly forgotten in the cultures where they have become just another item for the table, for the tongue.

This book guides both the novice, someone yet to experience this type of food preparation, and the professional who knows that to truly master and obtain consistent results in flavoring and preserving food products is to go back to the very basics — starting with good-quality raw ingredients and treating them with patience, respect, and just a little bit of flair that really adds a new dimension to their taste and to your experience eating them.

Great cooks and chefs are not really gifted with any more special skills than anyone else, but they have practiced and shown commitment to experimentation. They like trying something a little bit different — a little tastier, more tender, less tart or bitter, more juicy, less everyday or homogenized than what you can purchase while "hunting" through the chiller section of your local supermarket.

The key guidelines are: keep it simple, enjoy the experiences and tastes, discuss, exchange ideas, laugh and socialize. And most of all, savor the tastes of your region and support your local food producers.

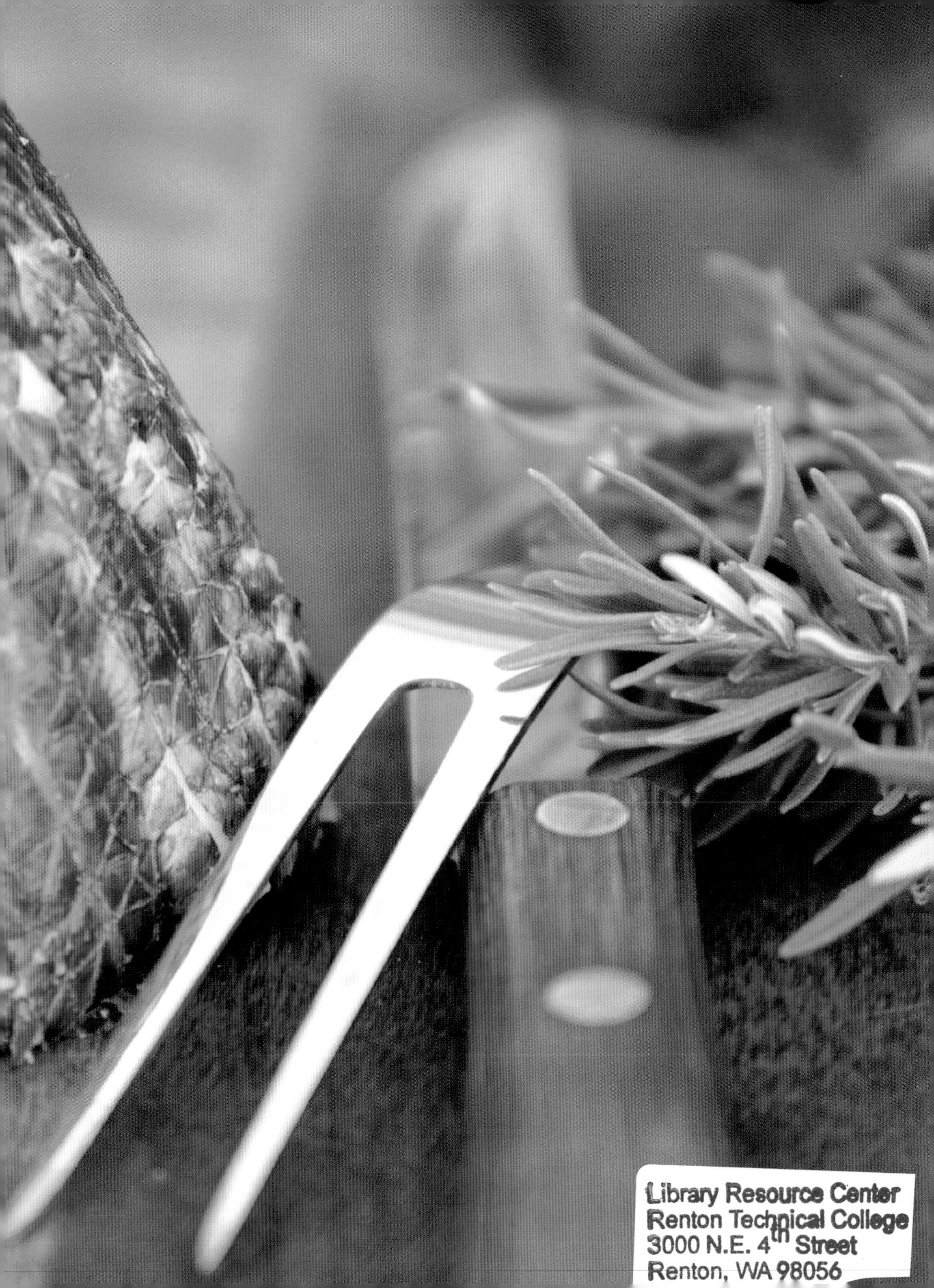

A micro-history of smoking: from hard necessity to fragrant flavor

The drying and smoking of fish and meats enabled different tastes and unusual foodstuffs to travel the world. Food trading introduced the preserved products of one culture to another and helped shape the world as we know it today. Smoking allowed food products to be shipped all around the globe for trade. And the products of smoking literally fuelled this trade by forming a staple part of the diet of the mariners shipping it — smoked food could last for months at sea while new frontiers, new markets, were explored. These products were not the smoked fish and meat we know today; the sailors' smoked fare was inedible unless soaked for many hours in water and then boiled to remove some of the tannic and smoky residues. Until the 1800s, heavily smoked fish and meat were the mainstays of European cuisine. This backbone of trade provided subsistence rations that helped people survive long, cold winters when food foraging was lean. With the development of railways, steamships and refrigeration, fresh animal produce was sent to markets and the popularity of smoking and drying declined. Smoking for preserving is no longer a way of life — but smoking for flavor is! Anybody with a barbecue, gas smoker, hot box, or set of old roasting tins can now enjoy the simplicity of smoking at home and the taste and flavor that smoked foods bring to the table.

The ways of smoking

Hot smoking

This is the more widely recognized and practiced method of smoking today and the majority of smokers that you can buy commercially are intended for this use.

Hot smoking flavors and cooks the food so that it can be consumed straight away. You can hot smoke seafood, meats, cheese, vegetables and even fruit. Hot smoking will not preserve the food because you don't remove enough moisture in the process, so anything you hot smoke should be refrigerated and treated exactly as you would other perishable products. This method of cooking and smoking is achieved by applying sufficient smoke and heat to the product, which normally means temperatures between 160°F and 360°F. It is an easier process than cold smoking and you can go from uncooked product to delicious treat in only 15 minutes. The time it takes to smoke and cook something depends on the amount of smoke flavor you want and the size and density of the food item.

Cold smoking

The cold smoking process preserves food in two steps: salt is added to remove excess moisture, then the food is subjected to a long, slow smoking period. However, the product is not cooked, so further cooking may be required before eating. Salmon and fish roes are two common cold-smoked items that do not require further cooking, however bacon, also delicious smoked this way, does need further cooking. Cold smoking is achieved by keeping the temperature of the food below 86°F for 6–32 hours depending on the final product. The heat source is generally kept well away from the product; however modern smokers can be turned right down for good cold-smoking temperatures.

Smoking essentials

Smoking a product does not offer a way to preserve or use food that is flawed or past its best-by date. It is essential that you use only the freshest and best-quality seafood, meats, vegetables, and fruits. The final, smoked product is determined by what goes into the smoker and the care and attention that it receives.

Sugar and salt are common ingredients in curing and brining. You can successfully hot smoke without using either, but they do aid the process and the right combination of sweet, sour, and bitter makes the real difference between average and exceptional smoked food. Herbs and

spices give extra depth and characteristics to the product but are not essential as smoking has its own particular strength of flavor and taste.

Pre-smoking processes
Curing
This is the process in which you use a brine or salt to remove moisture and stop the formation of bacteria. It also enhances the flavor.

Brining
The simplest way you can improve your smoked food products is by brining them. The food is submerged for a set amount of time in water or fruit juice and salt with added spices or herbs. The brine can either be strong or weak depending on the initial product and the desired effect. Simple brine is normally a 16:1 ratio of water to salt with the addition of sugar or spices to create a finer tasting product. Meat or fish is placed in the brine, depending on thickness, for 2–24 hours prior to smoking. Fillets of fish will take approximately 30 minutes to 2 hours to brine while a whole 4½ lb fish, butterflied, will benefit from being brined for 3–8 hours or even overnight. The general rule of thumb for

brining meat and poultry is approximately 1 hour for every 2 lb 3 oz of raw product. Keep the product submerged by placing a weight on top, then remove, rinse and dry before introducing it to the smoker. The thicker and denser the product the longer it will need to brine, but the final results will be well worth the extra effort and time. For an example of an easy brine that delivers a mouth-watering product see the recipe for Hot-smoked Salmon on Cucumber with Garlic Dressing on page 49.

Salting

A quicker method of curing is to use a strong salt mix, which is applied to draw out moisture. Sugar, pepper, herbs, or honey can be added to enhance the taste and counteract the intense salt flavor. Prior to smoking, the meat or fish is rubbed with salt and any other spices, allowed to sit for 2–24 hours and then washed and dried before the smoke is introduced. Thicker and denser items will benefit from being pressed during salting as this helps dry out moisture. Experiment with different types of sugar (e.g. brown sugar for darker results) and spices (e.g. star anise for an aniseed flavor). Salting allows the smoked flavor to be better absorbed by the food product because the reduced moisture in the food stops the thinning-out of flavor. Salting is part of the process in the recipe for Hot-smoked Wild Venison on page 57.

Marinating

This pre-cooking procedure combines spices and wet ingredients, such as oils, vinegars, or citrus, to flavor and tenderize. Some marinades can be added before smoking while others work better when applied a short time after smoking, just before the food is consumed. This is an easy way to enhance the taste of the final product — it can be as simple as brushing with Worcestershire sauce and leaving to sit for 30 minutes prior to smoking or cooking. Meats marinate well and benefit from being brushed with vegetable oil and sprinkled with fresh thyme or bay leaves to bring out their natural flavors. See the recipe for Hot-smoked Beef Fillet on page 57.

Dry rubbing

A combination of spices and salt is rubbed and massaged into the food before cooking to help seal in flavor, augment taste and soften the texture. These marinades can be left on while smoking takes place or, if using a delicate food item (shellfish or white fish), they may be washed off.

Dry rubbing is a more delicate procedure than salting and is undertaken to add flavor and extract moisture. You can purchase a range of speciality dry rubs but they are simple to make and store in the freezer or pantry for when you want to add that extra zing to a dish. By adding simple flavors before smoking and cooking you enhance the whole taste experience of the food. Hot-smoked Trout with Minted Yogurt, on page 50, uses a dry rub marinade to enhance the flavor of a favorite freshwater fish.

Air drying

Hanging meat or other foodstuffs in a safe box or the open air allows moisture to evaporate; the less moisture there is, the better the flavor and the faster the cooking. You can split fish down the middle and peg them to a line, or nail to a plank, so that air passes freely around it, or speed up the process by using a fan or place the food near an extractor fan. You can air dry from 30 minutes to 6 hours, and the benefits are certainly obvious in the final product. Doing the simple preparatory things well makes the smoking process easier and the taste of the food more satisfying.

Your smoker

You can purchase a variety of smokers nowadays as well as accessing information and plans on how to build your own. As with all things, start small and develop confidence before moving to the next step — practice makes perfect and there is no right or wrong when it comes to types and sizes of smokers. What type you choose will depend on what you want to achieve. Some of the best smokers I have used are nothing more than two old roasting tins with an improvised rack in the middle and a heat source underneath. The following smokers all vary in operational tricks and techniques. Make sure that you read the instruction manual first.

Compact stainless steel smokers

These compact and safe smokers are the most commonly available. They burn denatured alcohol, which is economical and easy to use. Any sort of wood chips can be burned in them and most are big enough to hold a good quantity of food. The hot smoke generated cooks food quickly, making these ideal for any product where cooking time is a factor. As with all smokers, you should prime it (i.e. give it a dry run) before your first smoking session. This removes any odors or residues that may be on the smoker. Denatured alcohol burners are the preferred heat source but these smokers work just as well over small gas rings. Line the bottom with tin foil for easy removal of charcoal or embers after use.

Kettle or hinged-lid barbecue smokers

It is easy to convert your barbecue into a good smoking unit, although you will be left with smoke odors for a few days afterwards, which may affect other cook-ups.

Charcoal, or gas, heat a smoke box (a metal case for the wood chips) while the food is placed on the racks.

To control the speed at which the wood chips burn you can soak a percentage of them prior to lighting to give a longer and slower burn time. The heat and barbecue lid acts like an oven, and provides a hot-smoking environment that is ideal for larger cuts of meat or poultry.

Food from one of these smokers is excellent eaten straight away. Easy-to-set smoke boxes can be purchased from most good retailers. Each barbecue and kettle will be different in terms of where you place the smoke box and the amount of heat generated. It may be useful to add a water tray to the barbecue to prevent food items from drying out. Most modern, hooded barbecues are fitted with temperature gauges that allow you to control the heat source by switching off one or two gas bars. If you are not comfortable with cooking for long periods of time or are a beginner, purchase a meat probe that tells you when poultry and joints of meat are cooked to perfection.

Cold smokers

Often custom-designed or home-made, cold smokers (which can vary from 44-gallon drums to old refrigerators or driers) give good food smoking results. They are often built with the materials at hand and can be custom-made to size to suit your own requirements. This gives the more adventurous smoker/cook the satisfaction of being able to smoke and preserve a great variety and quantity of food. For larger cuts of meat and fish, a much longer, more subtle smoking over a period of hours or days lets the smoke penetrate the item without overpowering it. Instead, the smoke flavor complements the food's natural flavors and helps in the preserving process.

For traditional cold-smoking, the heat source is located away from the product and then channelled into the hanging or racking chamber to give flavor. Different sawdusts, woods and shavings give results far superior to commercial additives and preservatives. Cold smokers are normally larger and not as transportable as other types of smokers and you need to keep a eye on the internal temperature to ensure that you are not heating the product above 100°F.

Water smokers

You can turn any hot smoker into a water smoker by adding a large tray of water to keep the final product moist and succulent. There is no need to flavor the water, which evaporates, so any spices or flavorings need to be in the brine or wood chips. Water smokers work well in keeping lean products, such as white game meats (rabbit, quail) and soft and delicate fish, moist while smoking. Using boiling water in the pan helps speed up the evaporation process.

Gas smokers

Gas smokers are perfect all-round smokers that allow you to both cold-smoke and hot-smoke, and they have good racking and hanging areas for the food product. They can easily be moved and are an ideal addition

to your outdoor cooking area. Gas smokers are designed for outdoor use only and should not to be used in a building, garage, or any other enclosed areas. The gas bottle should be switched off at the main tap after use and you should check all gas fittings with soapy water to detect any leaks prior to lighting. Ensure that the door is open before lighting the smoker to avoid any gas build-up and extreme care should be taken with naked flames. The smoker should be set up on a flat surface with plenty of ventilation around it. If you smell gas then immediately shut off the supply at the main valve. Extinguish any open flames and open door to smoker. Check all fittings and hoses for leaks and retest with soapy water.

Gas smokers are easy to use and enable you to hot or cold smoke by adjusting the temperature gauge and the internal thermometer. Plenty of space is available to smoke a large range of foodstuffs, which can either be placed on the racks or hung from the top shelf. An ignition switch allows for easy lighting of the smoking fuel, and you don't have to worry about overcooking food or drying it out because you can control the heat as in an oven. If you are serious about smoking and want to expand your culinary repertoire, then the gas smoker is certainly right for you.

Smoking basics
Smoking materials – different woods for very different flavors

Smoking material will vary depending on where you are and what is at hand. The ultimate is, of course, to use your own wood supply, but there are now stocks of different types of fuels that can be bought in good camping and outdoor stores. You could also talk to your local furniture makers and lumber yards to see what different types of wood varieties they can offer.

Alder
Delicate and good for smoking fish. Is also an all-rounder for pork, poultry and game birds.

Almond
A sweet and nutty flavored smoke that goes well with all meat products.

Apple
Produces a sweet, fruity taste. It is a good mild wood that works well on poultry, ham, beef, and game.

Cherry
Similar to apple. Sweet and usually very fruity depending on the age of the wood. Tends to be mild, which makes it a good choice for poultry, fish, and ham.

Grape vines
Aromatic and similar to other fruit woods. Excellent with all meats, wild and farmed.

Hickory
Probably the best-known wood. Can be quite pungent. Great for bacon and other dense products.

Maple
Gives a light and sweet taste which best complements poultry and ham.

Oak
A good choice for larger cuts that require longer smoking times.
Produces a strong smoke flavor but is usually not overpowering. Good
for brisket and other thick cuts of meat.

Walnut
A heavy smoking wood that can be mixed with lighter woods. Goes well
with stronger red meats and game.

Other flavoring materials

Some of the best flavors are produced by materials other than wood, such as tea leaves, rice, corn husks and spices. The following tables offer some excellent non-wood materials to use, either when preparing food or as an addition to your main fuel.

SPICE	FLAVOR	RECOMMENDED USE
Allspice	The dried, aromatic pimento berry, which provides a mixture of flavors, including nutmeg, cinnamon and cloves	Whole in brining solutions or crushed and added to rubs
Aniseed	Licorice flavor and aroma	Goes very well with seafood and subtle game meats
Caraway	Peppery, slightly bitter and warming	Is a must in smoked sausages and cheeses and works well in rubs
Cardamom	Lemony and bittersweet	Works well with salmon and in brines
Chili	Peppery	Add to your smoking chips or brine for extra flavor
Cloves	Sweet, pungent, and tangy	Used whole in brines and pickles
Coriander or cilantro	Mild and sweet with notes of sandalwood in the seeds	Mixed with other spices to make flavorsome rubs and brines
Cumin	Aromatic and strong	Great in marinades and brines or as a rub
Ginger	Rich and hot with real pungent warmth	Works well with chicken and fish
Juniper	Sweet, gin-flavored, and aromatic	Pickling and brines especially venison and red meats
Mixed spice	A mix of other spices including cinnamon, cloves, allspice	Goes well with fruit
Mustard seed	Mild and warming	Used whole in brines and rubs
Paprika	Sweet and peppery	Gives a smoky taste and color
Pepper	Pungent and spicy	Essential spice for meats

HERB	FLAVOR	RECOMMENDED USE
Basil	Pungent and sweet herb	Lamb, tomatoes and chicken are most partial to this herb
Bay leaf	Aromatic and proud	Can be mixed with smoking material or used in brines
Chervil	Delicate and fragrant	The queen of herbs; goes with seafood and white game meats
Dill	Sharp and fragrant, sweet	Essential with salmon and seafood in rubs or brines
Fennel	Aniseed and very fragrant	Chicken and vegetables partner well
Garlic	Pungent, strong, and aromatic	Works well with all products
Lemongrass	Lemony, strong, and flavorsome	Seafood and white meats, mixed with smoking materials
Marjoram	Spicy and sweet with strong musty aromas	Mixed with brines and spices for game products
Mint	Refreshing and revitalizing	Rubs and brines for lamb and vegetable
Oregano	Spicy sweet and lasting	Match with seafood and light red meats
Parsley	Common and mild with refreshing over-notes	Works well with most food products
Rosemary	Strong and pungent	Good for smoking with or adding to brines
Sage	Pungent and deep in aroma	Eat with chicken, venison, mushrooms
Tarragon	Flavorsome and cleansing	Combines with game and stronger seafood
Thyme	Coarse and pungent	Match with lamb, beef, pork and sausage

Storing smoked food

All food products that are not preserved by salting are best eaten as soon as possible and require refrigeration. Some smoked meats will taste better the day after as the flavors will have had time to develop and mature.

Refrigerate all perishable items for their normal recommended shelf life. It is wise to keep smoked items in an airtight container because the aroma will affect other food in the refrigerator, especially milk, cheese and eggs. Some cold-smoked products will have an extended shelf life of up to three weeks but they must still be refrigerated.

Wrapping in newspaper or vacuum packing and then freezing will allow products to be kept up to 12 months in the freezer. Before freezing break the food down into meal-sized portions, label, and put the current date on the package for future reference.

Frequently asked questions

Why won't smoking preserve the foods?
Smoking alone does not preserve because it does not inhibit the growth of bacteria inside the food. Preservation can be only achieved through drying, curing, or salting, which removes excess moisture.

Is smoked food good for you?
Everything in moderation — including moderation! Naturally smoked goods that contain preservatives and additives should be treated like all other food products and eaten in moderation. Artificial smoke flavors that are now found in a lot of commercial smoked goods need to be treated with some caution — research is still being conducted on the issues of long-term use and high consumption of these products.

Besides flavoring what else does smoking do to food products?
Smoke acts as an antioxidant in items that have been dried or salted. Oily
fish (salmon, kipper) benefit from this, hence their world-wide popularity.

Why brine before smoking?
Brining removes excess moisture and thus allows smoke to be easily
drawn into the product. It helps with the final flavor and firmness.
Brining is not essential for small pieces of short runs of smoking.

What are the ingredients in commercially produced "smoke" flavor?
Naturally-made smoke flavor is created using the same process as
traditional smoking. Wood or sawdust is burnt and the smoke is
captured through a retort system that processes and stabilizes the
particles. This should not to be confused with artificial smoke flavor that
is chemically made and should be avoided.

How long will cold-smoked fish last without refrigeration?
You should refrigerate cold-smoked products. Cold smoking will extend the
storage life of the product, but it is still best eaten as "fresh" as possible.

What is the best heat source to use when hot smoking?
Most small portable smokers will use denatured alcohol as the heat source
and although there is no control over the amount of heat generated you do
learn how to manage this with time and practice. Gas and electricity offer
more control and produce a better, more consistent product.

*Can I use white wine as the liquid in my water smoker to give
more flavor?*
When the liquid is heated the steam will rise leaving any flavor behind
in the pan so it makes no difference to the final product, but by using
white wine or juice in the brine you "inject" flavor into the product.

What is the difference between using brown sugar and white sugar?
For a darker and richer color in a final product such as salmon or dark
fish use brown sugar in your brines or cures. This gives a richer and
earthier cure than white sugar.

Can I brine in a bucket of seawater?
At about 3.5 percent, seawater does not contain enough salt for brining.
To effectively brine the solution should be roughly 20 percent salt (an
approximate water to salt ratio of 16:1) — enough to float a raw egg in.

Why use hard woods for smoking chips?
Hard woods are denser (they contain less moisture) and give more flavor
and aroma. They burn slower in all types of smoking material — from
planks to sawdust. Soft woods such as pine and firs contain resin and
gum.

*Can I use treated/preserved wood shavings or chips from the workshop
or sawmill?*
No. This wood contains toxic chemicals that will penetrate into the food
if it used for smoking material. Always purchase smoking chips from a
reputable supplier or personally know the source of the raw materials.

The do's & don'ts of smoking

There are no hard and fast rules for smoking, but common sense and keeping it simple prevail. Experimenting and making do with the resources that you have are all part of what makes the experience of smoking food enjoyable. The wise person learns from other people's mistakes; the smart person learns from his own mistakes; the stupid person never learns at all.

Do

1. Use the freshest and best quality ingredients possible to get the best finished result.

2. Use water in the drip tray when smoking products with very little fat, e.g. rabbit, venison, and chicken. Salmon, pork, and beef all contain good fat/protein ratios that prevent them from drying out excessively when smoking.

3. Experiment with different brining times and spices for each product — the ultimate test is your own taste buds.

4. Use hygienic and safe food preparation techniques. Smoking and curing foods is only as safe as the practices that you employ. Ensure that all perishable food is kept refrigerated and covered at all times. The use of a food thermometer will help monitor the internal cooking temperature of large cuts of meat. Make sure that you use different chopping boards and food platters for preparing raw and cooked meats to avoid cross-contamination.

5. Mix twigs and leaves of fruit woods such as apple, pear, or cherry to give more flavor and aroma. Spices and seeds such as juniper, star anise, and cardamom also add interesting tastes and aromas.

6. Allow time for drying the product before smoking it as this will give you a firmer, better-looking finished product.

7. Keep a recipe book and note pad handy to record each process so that you have a written history of what was successful.

8. Use an oven thermometer inside your hot smoker so that you know at which temperature the food is being cooked at — too hot and seafood will dry out; too cold and meats won't cook correctly.

9. Take the time to understand and learn about cold smoking as this particularly suits certain food products.

10. Enjoy and have fun. As soon as it becomes hard work, it all becomes too difficult.

But

1. Don't rush cold smoking techniques, as time is of the essence here.
2. Don't use treated, preserved, or varnished wood shavings or chips for smoking, or chemical cleaners to clean the inside of your smoker.
3. Don't mix fish and meat in the same salt brines or keep your salt brines longer than needed.
4. Don't smoke fish with other types of food — separate for best results.
5. Don't have products touching each other in the smoker. This prevents proper circulation of the smoke and produces patchy coloring.
6. Don't expect this time to taste and work out exactly like last time — different parameters will affect each batch.
7. Don't be put off curing by the anti-salt brigade.
8. Don't use salt with additives including iodine, anti-caking or magnesium. Good quality sea salt is best.
9. Don't allow excessive build-up of ash in the smoker — remove and clean each time.
10. Don't think that you have mastered it! Most cooks spend a lifetime mastering the techniques and processes of everyday food preparation even when 95 percent of the work has been done for them.

So, what went wrong?

The greatest mistake you can make in life is to continually fear that you are making one.

PROBLEM	SOLUTION
Not enough smoke flavor	Increase the amount of wood or burning material and leave longer
Fish is dark and bitter	Decrease the wood or burning material and decrease the time in smoker
Product too salty	1. Decrease the salting and brining time or use thicker cuts of product, or: 2. Add sugar to your brining or curing mix and ensure that you wash it off before smoking
Hot-smoked product not cooked	Increase the heat source or use thinner cuts of product so it cooks quicker
Vegetables are off-color and bitter tasting	Decrease the wood or burning material and decrease the cooking temperature
Poultry has a mushy texture to the flesh	Ensure that the product is dry before smoking
Product is dry and hard	Use a water tray in the smoker to raise humidity level
Smoke overpowers the taste of the product	Use a lighter smoking medium
The color of the final product is faded	Use brown sugar instead of white sugar to give better color retention
Meat has been cured with salt and sugar but has a slimy feel and look to it	Reduce the amount of sugar in the cure

Glossary of terms

Age
To hang meat before or after curing; reduces the moisture content and increases the flavor. Most red meats will benefit from aging from 3–21 days.

Botulism
A type of deadly food poisoning caused by dangerous levels of bacteria that produce a toxin. Botulism is normally related to canned goods or meats that have not been salt cured or processed correctly.

Brine
Curing medium for meats and fish consisting of salt or salt and sugar. Other flavors and spices can be added. Brines draw out moisture and allow smoke to be absorbed better.

Cold smoking
To smoke at a low temperature without cooking. A maximum temperature of 100°F allows the product to draw in smoke but not cook. Gives a longer shelf life but the product needs to be cooked prior to eating (except for some fish such as salmon).

Cure
A dry or wet mixture consisting of salt and/or sugar and other ingredients that draws out the moisture content and concentrates the flavor.

Honey cure
Can be used instead of sugar in a cure; bacon is the most common item that benefits from honey curing.

Hot smoking
To smoke and cook at the same time; allows the product to be consumed straight away.

Meat thermometer
Measures the internal temperature of cooked items; is placed inside the product to indicate the correct cooked temperature.

Pellicle
Shiny layer that is formed on the surface of products that have been soaked in a brine and then dried; improves the final appearance of the product.

Pickling salt
Used specifically for curing and brining; contains no iodine.

Potassium nitrate
Commonly known as saltpeter (an ingredient of gun powder); has now been banned from use in commercially cured meats.

Salmonella
A bacteria that causes food poisoning; produced in food products at a certain temperature range with moisture. Poultry and fish meat and eggs are the main cultivating agents; also kitchen items such as unclean chopping boards and bench tops.

Salt (sodium chloride)
Used as a seasoning and preservative; comes in many different formats and grains. The best salt to use for brining and curing in the smoking process is unrefined sea salt with no additives or anti-caking agents.

Sodium nitrate
Found in commercial meat cures; is very toxic and only very small amounts are used. Sodium nitrate has antimicrobial properties when used as a food preservative and can be found naturally occurring in green leafy vegetables. Colors meat pink and prevents it from browning. Commonly used in corned beef, hot dogs, and bacon. Has been linked to various types of cancer and consumption should be limited.

Sugar cure
Used like a salt cure; gives good color and helps break down tougher cuts of meat. Too much sugar will make the meat product feel slimy.

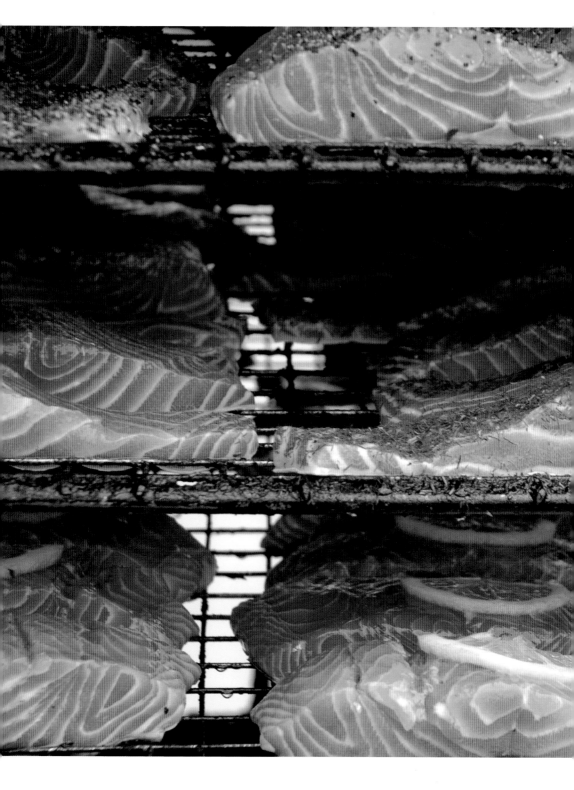

RECIPES:
BASIC & ADVENTUROUS

When smoking any foods, controlling the heat is an important part of the process: too hot and the product will overcook and dry out, too cold and it won't cook at all. Small portable hot smokers that sit over a denatured alcohol burner or gas flame are good for smoking small batches of food, but do not have the benefit of a controlled temperature gauge, so more care must be taken not to overcook the food. Most modern hooded barbecues are fitted with temperature gauges that make it easy to control the temperature by adjusting the heat source. If you are not comfortable with cooking for long periods of time or are a beginner, it is recommended that you buy a meat probe that allows you to tell when poultry and meats are cooked to perfection.

Before you get started – a few tips
- Basting with flavored liquids, or spraying with water, will add flavor and maintain a moist and succulent product.
- If you use an oven thermometer, you can tell what is happening in the smoker and adjust the heat accordingly.
- All recipes are dependent on variables: how fresh the product is; if it was brined and for how long; the thickness of the meats or fish; and the amount of wood chips or fuel that you use.
- Wood chips come in many different grades and sizes: the finer the sawdust or chip the faster the burn rate.
- Coarse wood chips are more suited for longer smoking periods and by soaking them in water prior to use you will get a more intense and pronounced smoke flavor. You can soak the wood in water for 1–12 hours depending on the thickness of the chips.
- Experiment by soaking all or 50 percent of the burning material, and using red wine or whiskey for different smoke flavors.
- Remember to use only natural wood chips that have not been chemically treated.

FISH & SEAFOOD

Smoking fish is one of life's simple yet great pleasures, experienced when you have either caught the fish yourself, or you have sourced it very fresh from your local fish market or seafood supplier. But there is really nothing better than catching your own and smoking it to perfection for all to share. Types of fish that smoke better than others are oily or fatty fish, such as mackerel, salmon, and kingfish but all fish will smoke well as long as you don't overcook them. Fresh is always best and if you are catching your own, you need to butterfly-fillet or fillet them before smoking. See pages 44–45.

Hot-smoked snapper or white fish

By controlling the temperature of the smoker you ensure that you do not overcook the delicate snapper fillets. A deep tanned color will form and the small pin bones will begin to stand proud as the snapper cooks.

1 whole snapper
¾ cup sea salt
1 cup brown sugar
1 tablespoon ground black pepper
3 cups smoking chips

Butterfly the fish as described on page 44, rinse, and pat dry. Mix salt, sugar and pepper together and spread on the flesh of the fish. Refrigerate for 2–3 hours. Rinse the fish and pat dry. Leave in a cool place with good air flow for 30 minutes to allow the flesh to dry out. Place on the smoker rack and smoke over a medium heat for 25–40 minutes or until the flesh is cooked and flakes easily with a fork.

To butterfly-fillet a fish

Work a sharp knife down both sides of the bones so you can remove them and split the fish open, but leave it whole with the skin on – this works well with small fish. Leaving the skin on when you smoke the fish protects the flesh and also helps prevent it from drying out – and it is easy to remove once it is cooked.

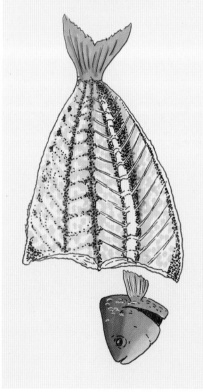

Filleting a fish

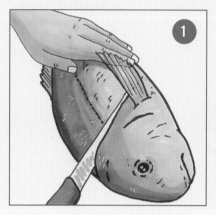

1. Make a cut just behind the gills (halfway through the thickness of the fish).

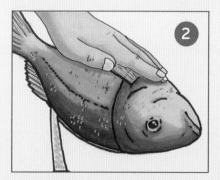

2. Cut a slit a few inches in length along the top of the fish (the dorsal side).

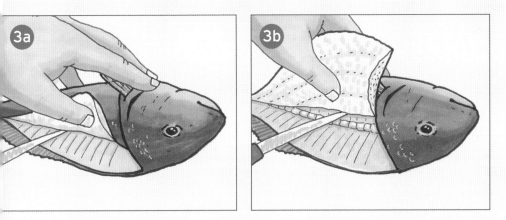

3. Using the tip of the knife, separate the flesh from the bones, as illustrated (3a). The fish should open up just like a book (3b).

4. When completely open, finish cutting away the fillet by moving the knife along the "spine of the book."

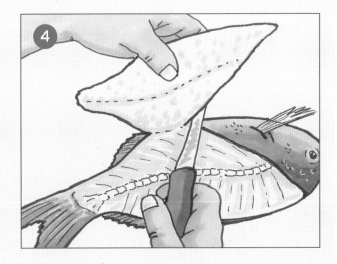

Basic cured & hot-smoked white fish

By gently curing and then smoking fillets of white fish you create a satisfying and tasty snack or meal that can be enjoyed with crusty bread any time of the day.

2½ cups water
¼ cup sea salt
2 tablespoons white sugar
zest and juice of one lemon
6½ lbs fish fillets, skin on
2 cups wood chips soaked in water for 30 minutes and drained

Mix the water, salt, sugar, and zest together and submerge the fish pieces in the brine. Refrigerate overnight. Remove from the brine and pat dry. Place on smoking rack and smoke over a low heat for 40–60 minutes or until cooked and translucent.

Smoked fish cakes

Perfect for using the leftover trimmings and end pieces of your smoked fillets, fish cakes are a universal favorite.

3 large baking potatoes
1 lb skinless, boneless smoked fish, flaked
2 large eggs, beaten
4 tablespoons unsalted butter, melted
½ cup coarsely chopped garden chives
¼ cup finely chopped flat leaf parsley
½ teaspoon sea salt
¼ teaspoon freshly ground pepper
1 cup fine fresh breadcrumbs
grape seed oil for frying

Steam or roast the potatoes for about 35 minutes, until tender. Allow
to cool, then peel and pass through a ricer or coarse sieve. In a bowl,
combine the potatoes, smoked fish, eggs, butter, chives, parsley, salt,
and pepper. Shape into 16 patties and crumb with breadcrumbs. Pan-fry
until golden brown in the grape seed oil. Serve hot with freshly made
salad or hand-cut potatoes.

Hot-smoked salmon on cucumber with garlic dressing

Traditional, tasty, and satisfying. The coolness of cucumber cuts through the richness of salmon cooked in a smoker. Adding capers and a garlic dressing makes this an irresistible meal.

Brining and cooking the salmon

3 quarts water
1 cup brown sugar
1 cup sea salt
3 lemons, sliced
2 sides of salmon
2 cups smoking chips

Mix water, sugar, salt, and lemon. Submerge the salmon pieces in the brine for at least two hours. Rinse well, pat dry and place on a smoking rack.

Place 2 cups of smoking chips in the smoker and hot smoke for approximately 15–25 minutes or until the salmon is medium cooked.

Garlic dressing

3 egg yolks, beaten
3 teaspoons dried mustard powder
6 cloves garlic, crushed
1½ teaspoons sea salt
½ teaspoon ground black pepper
½ teaspoon dried oregano leaves
15 drops hot pepper sauce
5 tablespoons white vinegar
olive oil

Combine all dressing ingredients, except olive oil, in a blender using low speed. Maintain speed and add olive oil very slowly until mixture thickens and is the consistency of mayonnaise. Season to taste if required, refrigerate up to a week, using as needed.

Plating the salmon
1 cucumber
hot-smoked salmon pieces
2 tablespoons capers
dressing

Cut the cucumber in half and remove seeds. Peel cucumber flesh into long, thin strips. Place salmon pieces on top of the cucumber strips. Sprinkle with capers and drizzle over the garlic dressing.

Hot-smoked trout with minted yogurt

The hardest part of this dish is catching or sourcing the trout. Treat trout like salmon and you can't go wrong. Trout benefits from the smokiness of the wood chips and the tanginess of the herbed yogurt.

Seasoning and smoking the trout
3 cleaned, boned whole trout, heads and tails removed
2 tablespoons sea salt
¼ cup brown sugar
½ teaspoon fresh thyme leaves
1 teaspoon grated lemon zest
2 tablespoons grape seed oil
2 cups wood chips, soaked in water for 30 minutes and drained

To fillet the trout, start with the trout's back facing towards the edge of the table. This is the right fillet. Cut down behind the gill plate to the backbone. Follow the backbone all the way to the tail. Cut the ribs out

by pushing down on them so they are flat on the table, then cut under them and remove them. On the left side, make a cut from the back to the belly. With your knife tip, cut over the belly fin down to the anal fin. Follow the backbone all the way to the tail. Remove the ribs by cutting under them. The pin bones are removed by either using pliers to pull the bones out or by making two cuts on each side in a "V" shape.

Rinse trout fillets and pat dry. Mix salt, sugar, thyme, and lemon zest together. Gently rub onto fillets, cover and chill. Cure for 2–3 hours. Rinse the fillets with cold water to remove the salt and sugar. Brush with oil and place on racks. Smoke for 10–15 minutes or until just cooked.

Minted yogurt

2 cups firm Greek yogurt
2 cloves garlic, finely minced
¼ cup chopped parsley
¼ cup chopped mint
¼ cup chopped dill or fennel tops
juice and zest of 2 lemons
sea salt and pepper

Mix all ingredients together and chill in fridge for 1 hour. Serve in a dipping bowl with smoked trout.

Mussels hot smoked with bell peppers

Harvested straight from the ocean, there is no better way to enjoy mussels. They taste better when eaten while you sit around a fire at the beach.

1 cup wood chips
2 bell peppers (red, yellow, orange or green)
1 lemon
3 dozen live mussels in their shells, debearded and scrubbed
3 tablespoons olive oil

Soak the wood chips in water for approximately 30 minutes. Slice the pepper and lemon into quarters and place on a tray with the mussels. Smoke on a high heat until the mussels are open. Discard any that fail to open. Remove the mussels from their shells and combine with the olive oil, lemon and peppers. Serve with crusty bread. To make a tasty and easy dip, purée in a food processor with one cup of cream cheese and plenty of black pepper.

Hot-smoked oysters with tomato & chili salsa

A steady hand while shucking fresh oysters as well as a good smoking technique will add an extra layer of flavor to these tasty morsels. Perfect for the beachside or eating outdoors.

24 live oysters (unopened)
1 cup smoking wood of your choice

Shuck the oysters then place them back on their shells. Retain the juice from the oyster as this is its natural brine.

Place onto the smoking tray and smoke over a high heat for 4–6 minutes or until the oysters have absorbed enough smoke. Serve with a tomato and chili salsa or just as they are.

Tomato & chili salsa

5 tomatoes
juice of 1½ lemons
fresh hot red chili peppers or mild green chili peppers
½ red onion, finely chopped
2 tbsp chopped fresh coriander
sea salt and black pepper

Finely dice the tomatoes and mix with other ingredients. Season to taste and stir in the coriander.

Chilli Peppers
$1.00 each

RED MEATS
Hot-smoked beef fillet

Outdoor dining will never be quite the same again once you start eating you own smoked cuts of meat. Beef fillet absorbs smoke flavors very well. Take care not to overcook it and allow it to rest for as long as you can before serving. Serve with crushed potatoes and freshly picked salad greens.

4 beef fillet steaks, 5 oz each
4 tablespoons Worcestershire sauce
olive oil
sea salt and pepper
3 cups wood chips, soaked in water and drained

Marinate the seasoned fillets in the Worcestershire sauce for 30 minutes, then brush with olive oil and place on smoking racks. Smoke over a high heat for 15 minutes or until the meat is cooked to your liking. Allow to rest in a warm place, then slice and serve.

Hot-smoked wild venison

If you are lucky enough to be able to get wild venison loins or fillets then this is the perfect way to add flavor and taste. Using a dry salt and sugar method allows the meat to tighten and absorb a better smoke flavor.

Salt cure
½ cup brown sugar
⅓ cup sea salt
1 tablespoon ground black pepper

To smoke

Mix the ingredients together and spread evenly over the venison. Allow to rest for a minimum of one hour and up to four. Place in hot smoker and use your favorite wood chips. Hot smoke for 10 minutes and then allow to cool. In a hot frying pan or on a barbecue seal the meat very quickly. Cook until golden brown and then slice thinly and serve with horseradish or mustard.

Marinated, smoked rabbit

Rabbit is a dry meat with very little fat so marinating it overnight will help keep it tender and moist. Or try brining it with water, salt, herbs, and spices before placing in the smoker.

> ¾ cup olive oil
> 1 cup cider vinegar
> juice of two lemons
> 2 teaspoons salt
> 1 teaspoon coarsely ground pepper
> 2 cloves garlic, minced
> 4 rabbit quarters
> 2 cups of wood chips soaked in water for 2 hours

Combine all ingredients, add the rabbit quarters, and marinate overnight, turning several times. Put the marinated rabbit on a grill rack and place in the smoker. Smoke for 2–4 hours at 320°F or until the meat shreds away from the bone. Do not overcook/smoke as rabbit is a delicate meat, and it will dry out and become chewy.

Hot-smoked spicy sausages

You'll never have boring or bland sausages again. Use home-made pork or beef sausages or ask your local butcher for the finest they have. These take no time at all and turn the ordinary into the sublime — all with very little effort.

1½ cups smoking chips
2 dozen thick or thin spicy sausages

Hang the sausages in the fridge or in front of a fan to dry their skins. This allows them to absorb the smoke better. Soak half of the wood chips for 20 minutes and drain. Place sausages on racks and smoke for 30 minutes on a high heat. Finish cooking on the barbecue grill if necessary — ensure that they are cooked all the way through before serving.

Butterflied leg of hot-smoked lamb with rosemary sprigs

A robust and wholesome dinner of smoky lamb laced with rosemary and garlic that is so delicious there may not be much left over for the next day!

1 leg of lamb, deboned and butterflied
6 sprigs rosemary
4 cloves garlic, slithered
sea salt and pepper
3 cups smoking chips
½ cup red wine

Ask your butcher to butterfly the lamb for you, or do it yourself. Using a sharp knife, simply follow the length of the bone gently pulling back the meat as you go until it is completely free of the bone. It's not that hard, so give it a go!

With a sharp knife make small nicks in the lamb and stud with

rosemary and garlic slithers. Season well with salt and pepper and place on a tray. Soak the smoking chips in the red wine for 30 minutes and then drain. Place in the smoker and smoke on a medium to high heat. Use a thermometer to test the meat's internal temperature, which should be approximately 150°F. Remove from the smoker and allow to rest for 30 minutes before serving.

PORK & BACON
Pork ribs hot-smoked over oak

Finger-licking delicious, these are satisfaction guaranteed and perfect for any occasion. Take the time to marinate and smoke for as long as you can to get the full flavor of these ribs.

1 cup brown sugar
½ cup paprika
2½ tablespoons ground black pepper
2½ tablespoons sea salt
1 tablespoon medium mustard powder
1½ tablespoons chili powder
1½ tablespoons garlic powder
1½ tablespoons onion powder
1 teaspoon cayenne pepper
4½ lbs pork spare ribs
4–5 cups oak smoking chips soaked in water

Baste mixture
¼ cup olive oil
¾ cup cider vinegar

Mix ingredients together. Wet the ribs all over and then coat with the spice mix. Place ribs on a smoking rack and smoke over a medium heat for 2–3 hours or until cooked. Baste every 30 minutes to help retain moisture and add flavor.

Pork fillet hot smoked with mustard

4 pork fillets, 1 lb to 1½ lbs each
2 tablespoons sea salt
2 tablespoons brown sugar
1 teaspoon black pepper
1 teaspoon medium mustard powder
2 cups wood chips

Pat dry the pork fillets and then coat with sea salt, sugar, pepper, and mustard powder. Refrigerate for approximately 2 hours. Rinse and dry. Place on smoking rack and smoke over medium to high heat for 20–30 minutes or until juices run clear. Serve with wholegrain mustard or a plum sauce to add extra flavor to the pork fillet.

Dry-cured hot-smoked bacon

No artificial colors, water or unnecessary nitrates and chemicals are found in the bacon you can make using any home-made bacon recipe. You will never go back to mass-produced bacon again.

5½ lbs pork belly, rind removed
1 tsp sodium nitrite (ask your butcher)
¼ cup sea salt
½ cup maple syrup, brown sugar or honey
6 cups smoking chips

Rub the sodium nitrite over both sides of the meat and repeat with the salt and syrup/sugar/honey. Place in a large zip lock bag and refrigerate. Turn daily. After five days, remove from the bag and wash well. Leave to dry in a meat box or the fridge for as long as possible — this will help the smoking process. Pat dry and place on a smoking rack.

Smoke in a cold smoker for 4–6 hours depending on how smoky you like your bacon. Store wrapped in muslin or hung in the fridge for good air circulation. Slice and cook.

Wet brine-smoked bacon

This is a 100 per cent natural cure without nitrites or nitrates.

>*2 quarts water*
>*1 cup salt*
>*¾ cup brown sugar, or molasses*
>*2 bay leaves*
>*3 cloves garlic, minced*
>*3 tablespoons cracked black pepper*
>*3 tablespoons crushed dried chili peppers*
>*9-11 lbs pork loin, skin removed*
>*5 cups wood chips (more if needed)*

Combine all the ingredients in a pot and bring to the boil, allow to cool. Immerse the pork in the cold brine and weigh down so that it is submerged. After three days, rinse, pat dry and place on smoking rack. Leave for 12–24 hours to allow for good smoke uptake. Smoke in a cold smoker for 4–5 hours, allow to set. Store wrapped in muslin cloth or hung in the fridge for good air circulation. Slice and cook.

CHICKEN & DUCK
Hot-smoked chicken & lemon thyme

This is a great smoked chicken recipe with a lot of lemon flavor! The key with whole chickens is that once cooked, allow them to rest for as long as you have cooked them — this will ensure they are succulent.

1 whole chicken
½ cup lemon juice
1 tablespoon sea salt
1 lemon, peeled
1½ cups breadcrumbs
2 cloves garlic
1 teaspoon black pepper
2 teaspoons lemon thyme
½ cup fruit wood chips

Clean chicken, rinsing inside and out with running water. Rub with lemon juice and salt. Mix breadcrumbs with garlic, pepper and lemon thyme. Stuff chicken with breadcrumbs and seal the cavity with the lemon. Place in hot smoker with preferred smoking chips. Smoke for

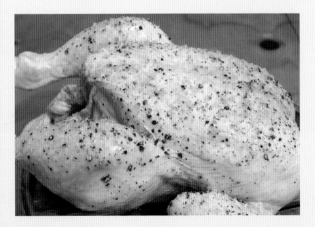

30 minutes or more depending on the depth of smoke flavor you want.

Remove and place in a hot oven or hooded barbecue to cook for a further 20–30 minutes or until the juices run clear. Allow to rest in a warm place for at least another 30 minutes before eating. This will ensure that the meat is tender.

Basic hot-smoked chicken

While brining does take a little longer, the results are well worth the extra time as you will be rewarded with juicy and succulent smoked chicken breasts.

1 tablespoon molasses or ¼ cup brown sugar
¼ cup salt,
4 cups water
dried or fresh herbs or spices to flavor the breasts — try tarragon,
    thyme, garlic (optional)
4 boneless chicken breasts with skin on (this helps protect the flesh
    while smoking)
2 cups smoking chips

Dissolve the molasses, or sugar, and salt in 2 cups of boiling water. Add the remaining 2 cups of cold water and allow to cool. Add optional spices and herbs and the chicken breasts. Cover and leave in brine for 12–24 hours. Remove and dry the breasts, place on smoking racks and smoke over a medium heat for 30–45 minutes or until cooked (the juices should run clear when a breast is pierced with a sharp knife). Serve hot or cold with your favorite salads and accompaniments.

Hungarian hot-smoked chicken

To make the best smoked chicken you need to allow time for the meat to soak in brine. This keeps it succulent and moist while drawing in the smoke flavoring.

3½ quarts cold water
1 cup sea salt
½ cup sugar
2 onions, diced
4 cloves
1 medium-sized whole chicken

Bring 1 quart of the water to the boil with salt and sugar, simmer for 2 minutes. Add remaining water, onions, and cloves. Split the chicken down the center and rinse before submerging in brine for 6–8 hours. Refrigerate. Remove from the brine and pat dry.

Rub

2 tablespoons onion powder
1 tablespoon white sugar
1 tablespoon paprika
2 teaspoons dried parsley
1 teaspoon garlic powder
1 teaspoon ground black pepper
grapeseed oil

Mix all the dry ingredients together thoroughly. Brush the chicken with grapeseed oil and then sprinkle on the rub. Place in the smoker for 2–3 hours at 250°F or until the juices run clear. Allow to rest for 30 minutes before serving.

Green tea smoked duck breasts

An easy and tasty way to prepare duck breasts, which benefit from being brined for several hours prior to smoking. Because duck contains very little fat the brine helps prevent them from drying out during smoking. This recipes works just as well with chicken breasts or any other game bird.

8 duck breasts

Brine
⅓ cup sea salt
8 star anise, chopped
6 bay leaves
1 quart water

Smoking mixture
1 cup white rice
5 tablespoons green tea
¼ cup granulated sugar

Trim the duck breasts of any excess fat and score with a sharp knife. Remove the silver skin and place in the brine for a minimum of 4 hours and preferably overnight. Remove from brine and dry well. Place on the smoking rack and seal. Set smoker to high for 5 minutes, then reduce the heat to medium for 10 minutes. Remove from the heat and allow to rest uncovered for 20 minutes. Slice and serve with crispy salad greens or new potatoes.

Cherry tree hot-smoked chicken wings

Marinated with honey and soy, kissed with smoke and served sticky
and hot — what more could you ask for?

½ cup light soy sauce
⅓ cup honey
1 lemon, zested and juiced
1 orange, zested and juiced
1 garlic clove, crushed
4½ lbs chicken wings
2 cups cherry tree wood chips, soaked for 10 minutes in orange juice

Combine soy sauce, honey, lemon juice and zest, orange juice and zest,
and garlic in a bowl. Mix well. Place the chicken wings in an ovenproof
dish in a single layer and pour the marinade over the top. Smoke for
30 minutes on a medium heat or until cooked. Can be placed on the
barbecue grill or into the oven to make sticky.

VEGETABLES

Hot-smoked corn on the cob

Removing some of the husk before smoking will allow the smoke to penetrate the kernels. Finish off on a hot grill if needed.

10 ears of corn, husks still on
4 cups smoking sawdust
olive oil
flaky sea salt and cracked black pepper

Open the corn husk and carefully remove the silk from the cob. Place in a large container of water and soak for 1–2 hours. Pull the husk back down over the ears of corn and smoke over a low heat for 1 hour. Remove from the smoker. Pull back the husk and brush with olive oil, salt, and cracked black pepper. Serve immediately.

Tea hot-smoked tomatoes

When tomatoes are in abundance this is the perfect way to increase flavor to a favorite summer dish. It's easy to prepare — and even easier to eat!

8 large tomatoes, halved
sea salt and pepper

Smoking mix
½ cup good quality tea leaves (try jasmine tea leaves or any
   strong-flavored loose-leaf tea)
1 cup raw rice
¼ cup soft brown sugar

Mix the smoking mix ingredients together and place into the hot smoker. Add your fuel and bring to a good smoking point. Place the rack of tomatoes on top. Smoke for approximately 10 minutes, then serve.

Smoky tomato ketchup

An old style version of this ever-essential condiment on the dinner table. Keep it in the fridge — if it lasts long enough!

11 lbs smoked tomatoes
½ cup sugar
2 tablespoons medium mustard powder
1 tablespoon ground allspice
2 cups cider vinegar
3 tablespoons salt
7 oz tomato paste
1 tablespoon black pepper
1 teaspoon ground cloves

Select good, ripe tomatoes. Smoke for 1 hour over a low heat, scald and strain through a coarse sieve or a small grater to remove seeds and skin. Add the remaining ingredients to the tomatoes and bring to the boil. Let simmer slowly for 2–3 hours. Pour into hot, sterilized jars.

Hot-smoked tomatoes

These tomatoes are best eaten straight away so that you don't lose the freshness and appeal of your effort.

12 large tomatoes
sea salt and pepper
olive oil
2 cups sawdust

Halve the tomatoes and place on a smoking tray. Sprinkle with sea salt and pepper and brush with olive oil. Over a low to medium heat, smoke the tomatoes for 30 minutes then remove and store in an airtight container or bag until needed. Can be added to soups and salads to give a real flavor boost.

Hot-smoked potato salad

This lightly smoked salad is ideal partnered with cold cuts of meat and preserves. Don't over-smoke the potatoes or they will take on the bitter flavors rather than the aromas of the wood chips.

21 oz potatoes, peeled and diced large
½ cup onion, chopped
½ cup gherkins, chopped
3 hard-boiled eggs, coarsely chopped
⅓ cup mayonnaise
2 tablespoons cider vinegar
1 tablespoon Dijon or English mustard
sea salt and pepper
fresh garden herbs
2 cups smoking chips or sawdust

Steam or boil potatoes until firm but just cooked. Drain and pat dry. Place on smoking rack and smoke over a low heat for 40–60 minutes. Remove from the smoker and roughly chop. Mix with remaining ingredients and chill.

Hot-smoked & whipped sweet potato & orange with sour cream

Delicate and light, this sweet potato whip is perfect made the day before and kept in an airtight plastic container or piping bag. The sweetness of the orange is a perfect partner for the sweet potato.

17 oz sweet potato
1 cup sour cream
2 oranges, segmented
chives, finely chopped
cracked black pepper

Peel the sweet potato and cut into even-sized pieces. Steam and then place on smoking rack. Smoke 5–8 minutes with your favorite wood chips and then allow to cool. Purée in a food processor, adding the sour cream and seasoning. Pipe onto crackers and top with an orange segment, sprinkle with chives and season with freshly cracked black pepper.

Hot-smoked pearl onions

Sweet baby onions are perfect smoked in their skins, then tossed with fresh thyme and served with barbecued meats.

3 dozen baby onions, skins on
5 sprigs of thyme
2 tablespoons olive oil
juice of one lemon
1 cup smoking chips, soaked for 10 minutes in water

Place the onions onto a smoking tray. Smoke on a high heat for 30–40 minutes or until tender. Remove from the smoker and peel. Toss with fresh thyme, olive oil, and lemon juice. Season to taste.

Cold-smoked garlic bulbs

The key to smoking garlic bulbs is to use fresh, firm garlic and smoke them for as long as you can at the coolest possible temperature. This will give them a shelf-life of up to three months. Otherwise you can hot-smoke them at 320°F for 1–2 hours, but they would need to be eaten within 4 days.

> *6 garlic bulbs*
> *3 cups of smoking chips soaked in water for 2–4 hours (add more*
> *chips as required)*

Place garlic bulbs on smoking racks and cold-smoke for 6–24 hours, or until you have the desired smoked flavor. Garlic bulbs should be a vibrant golden brown.

Black tea hot-smoked field mushrooms with garlic

Mushrooms hold the smoke flavor very well and because they contain so much water, they do not dry out. You can keep them longer by covering them with a very light vegetable oil and refrigerating.

> *9 oz field mushrooms, peeled*
> *4 large garlic cloves, finely chopped*
> *olive oil to coat mushrooms*
> *freshly ground black pepper*

Smoking mixture
> *½ cup dry rice*
> *¼ cup raw sugar*
> *½ cup loose black tea leaves*

Quarter or halve mushrooms, depending on their size, to make bite-size pieces and place in a bowl. Toss lightly to coat with the garlic, olive oil and black pepper. Place in hot smoker and smoke for approximately 5–8 minutes or longer if you desire a heavier smoke.

Red wine barrel hot-smoked mushrooms

This is one of my favorite ways to cook mushrooms. They absorb the wine and oak aromas, which go well with the earthy, musty taste of mushrooms.

> *½ cup of red wine barrel shavings*
> *3½ tbsp red wine*
> *12 field mushrooms, peeled*

Soak a quarter of the red wine barrel shavings in the red wine. Heat the remaining shavings to smoke point in your smoker. Add the soaked shavings and place the mushrooms on a rack above. Seal the smoker and hot smoke for 20 minutes or until the mushrooms are cooked. Allow to cool and serve with hot buttered toast or as a side of vegetables.

CHEESE

Cold-smoked cheese

You can try this with any type of cheese but cheddars and Colby will work best. With cold smoke you do not want any heat involved, otherwise you will have a molten mass of protein. Smoked cheese goes well as part of your main meal, or as an entrée, accompanied by relish or pickles.

> *2¼ lbs cheese, cut into quarters (the smaller the pieces the less time*
> *needed for smoking and the richer the flavor)*
> *1 cup strong wood smoke chips (such as cherry)*

Leave the quartered cheese out for a couple of hours so that it firms up — this will allow it to more easily absorb smoke. Place the cheese on racks inside your smoking box or barbecue. Cold-smoke at the lowest possible temperature for as long as you can, refilling the woodchips 2–3 times, depending on the strength of the smoke that you want in the cheese, to achieve the desired result.

OTHER TREATS

Hot-smoked chocolate & red wine

Don't be fooled by this simple recipe. It is certainly for the more adventurous foodie. Goes well by itself or served with refreshing sliced melon or cakes.

18 oz chocolate
1¼ cup cream
5 tbsp red wine

Grate chocolate into the cream and place into the smoker. Smoke over a low heat for 20 minutes, stirring every 10 minutes. Remove from the smoker and place over a pot of boiling water. Whisk and add red wine. Allow to cool, then serve.

Hot-smoked apricots

Smoked apricots, with their own sweet and juicy nectar enhanced by the smoke flavor, go well with pork and chicken dishes as well as cheese and cold cut meat platters.

10 apricots, firm but ripe
1 cup smoking chips

Halve the apricots and remove the stone. Place on a smoking rack and smoke over a low heat for 20 minutes. Turn off the smoker and allow the apricots to sit for 1 hour with the lid closed. Store in an airtight container or bag in the fridge until needed.

Hot-smoked lemons

Barbecued or grilled lemons maximize the fruit's flavor, and smoking imparts a wafting, zesty taste that is very refreshing.

8 lemons, sliced in half
1 cup smoking chips

With a sharp knife remove any seeds from the lemons and place on a smoking tray. Smoke over a low heat (no more than 212 °F) for 12–15 minutes. Remove and allow to cool. Serve with seafood dishes for that little extra flavor.

Hot-smoked apple sauce

Smoky apples go well with juicy, tender pork. The key to cooking pork loin or fillet is to make sure that you let it rest for as long as you have cooked it — this allows the juices to relax and the meat to be tender. Always rest the cooked meat in a warm place so that it does not go cold, then slice and serve it with this delicious apple sauce. Sauces and accompaniments work well with opposites (smoky with plain, sweet with sour) so use this sauce to add extra flavor to any pork dish.

6 Granny Smith apples, peeled and cored, cut into quarters
1 white onion, peeled
3 cloves of roasted garlic
½ cup smoking sawdust

Place apples and diced onion on a tray and smoke for 10 minutes. In a food processor, pulse the smoked apples and the roasted garlic until roughly chopped. Season to taste.

Hot-smoked spicy ginger peanuts

Perfect to keep on hand for a late-night snack or to mix through salads and sprinkle on top of stir-fries.

2 cups peanuts
2 teaspoons sesame or peanut oil
½ teaspoon ground ginger
½ teaspoon chili powder
1½ teaspoons sea salt or more to taste
1 cup wood chips

Mix together all the ingredients, except the salt, and place on a smoking tray. Smoke for 10–20 minutes in a hot smoker. Cool, sprinkle with sea salt and store in an air-tight container.

Hot-smoked almonds

Earthy, salty, crispy and addictive — the ultimate bar snack for the home cook. Also good with other nuts, such as cashews or hazelnuts, as well.

2 cups whole almonds
1 tablespoon olive oil
fine-grained salt to taste
1 cup smoking chips or
*   sawdust*

Mix almonds with olive oil and place on a smoking tray. Hot-smoke for 20–30 minutes, stirring several times. Remove and sprinkle with salt to taste. Store in an airtight container.

Hot-smoked crystal salt

When you require that special seasoning to give steaks and potatoes an extra lift, this strongly smoked rock salt will do the trick.

1 cup wood chips or sawdust
2 cups rock salt

Get the wood chips smoking in the smoker and place a tray of salt above them. Cover and smoke for approximately 1 hour or longer if you want a stronger smoke taste. Allow to cool. Store in an air-tight container.

Rock salt & spice smoke

Smoked salt with extra spice will add an instant flavor dimension to a meal — more spice for the more adventurous.

1 cup woodchips or sawdust
½ cup rock salt
2 tablespoons table salt
4 teaspoons sugar
1 teaspoon paprika
1 teaspoon turmeric
1 teaspoon onion powder
2 teaspoons garlic powder

Get chips smoking in the smoker and place a tray of salt above them. Cover and smoke for approximately 30 minutes or longer if you want a stronger smoke taste. Allow to cool then add remaining ingredients and store in an air-tight container.

Index

ALL YOU NEED TO KNOW TO CREATE YOUR
OWN DELICIOUS SMOKED FOODS.

smoking food, but for those with less experience, this book provides
information on getting started, including handy suggestions on how to
ed product. For those who are old hands at smoking, the wide range of
g recipes encourages you to get more adventurous with your smoker.
ortune has developed all these recipes to help you get the most out of
y his Hot-Smoked Oysters with Tomato and Chili Salsa or Hot-Smoked
. The Pork Ribs Hot-Smoked over oak are hard to beat, as are the Green
uck or Chicken Breasts. The vegetable section has versatile Smoky
p, and there are also delicious recipes for smoking cheese, nuts, and

d are the pre-smoking processes and smoking techniques: which
oose for different flavors — wood, spices, or herbs; information on
of smokers and how to use them; and how to store smoked food, along
oubleshooting guide.

is Fortune is a founding member of the Farmers' Market and slow food movements
nd in 2003 he won the New Zealand *Hell's Kitchen*. He is an advocate for honest,
nome-produced foods. www.chrisfortune.co.nz

ISBN 978-0-8117-1442-6

51695>

9 780811 714426

STACKPOLE
BOOKS

www.stackpolebooks.com

$16.95 U.S.
Higher in Canada
Printed in China